Names of God (1986)
From the Great Above She Opened
Her Ear to the Great Below (with Susan Shantz) (1988)
Tourist to Ecstasy (1989)
Moosewood Sandhills (1994)
Living In The World As If It Were Home (1999)
To the River (1999)
Kill-site (2003)
Going Home (2008)
Orphic Politics (2008)
Assiniboia (2012)
The Names (2016)
The Larger Conversation (2017)
The House of Charlemagne (2018)

# HARMONIA

# MUNDI

### TIM LILBURN

XYLEM BOOKS 2022

Tim Lilburn, *Harmonia Mundi*
First published in 2022 by Xylem Books

ISBN: 978-1-9163935-6-1

Xylem Books is an imprint of Corbel Stone Press

## The Philosophical History

*Actants, Conatus*

*The Philosophical History*

*by Priscianus*

*In 529, the emperor Justinian, supported by the official church, suppressed the Academy of Plato in Athens, and a particular form of knowing — theurgic, therapeutic, metaphysical — went underground. Priscianus was a member of a small party of philosophers, led by Damascius, who carried the Academy to the Persian court of Khusrau. They believed the young tyrant was an earnest student of Plato's works, but they soon discovered him instead to be cruel and prone to feverish swings in temperament.*

## Damascius's Ascesis, Ambulatory

His head in the mouth
of the way, he carries the machine
of the entire world-system
across the desert to the lord
on the far side of the River.
Lizard tongue   exfoliating
    winds. Non-stop.
Khusrau yammers from 8:00 P.M.
to 2:00 P.M. the following day.
Arrow fall questions with
breaks for igniting rockets
whose burned stalks courtiers
return with reports on their range.
Damascius fans on a court
carpet one ecstatic
recital then another, face down.
Khusrau's energy is insane.
There he runs
along the colonnades.

*Isidore, Pedagogue*

I saw the meteoric stone.
I saw the baetyl, its purple short quills.
The soul holds a luminous vehicle,
star-like, unbroken
in a sheath lodged in
some in their heads, others
in the right shoulder,
immaculate body that accompanies
                                    the soul,
sweeping in webby weight at its edges,
its warming pelt speed.
I saw the baetyl, which is not this body
but the oracle's clear, fixed mouth,
shifting in air, now sequestered,
covert in the clothes of its guardian, now
in the cup of Eusebius's hands.
This rock, I believe, is moderately wicked
in its short purple quills.
As I tell you this your soul grows
grey eyes.
Minus 45 degrees in these parts these nights
                            in this expanse of snow.
Men keep low fires roused below their
            fuelled conveyances through the dark hours.

(*Philosophical History* paras. 138, 153)

*A Mountain Floats Before Us*


We wake to see the dorsal crest of SN̲, AK̲E in just milked
luminosity, little more than night's moult: and a curly mass of wiry,
shaded nothing the mountain keeps in its abdominal trenches. This,
in its indifferentiation, we agree, is the support stone of wealth.

All streams coming off the mountain, weeping through moss or
        tumbling
along small, bouldered trails are invisible still. Battering wind,
new moon in and out of storm
front clouds. For a day we linger at this place then lift all we've
laid by the track and so we progress.

We had never heard of philosophy
so despised in Athens
as we saw it ribboned in the time of Hegias,
student of Proclus, diadochus of the 490s.
Now this.

The streets shook the enterprise in their teeth.
Monophysites and Chalcedonians, rogue
Swells, broke in shops and gardens of the city.

*Damascius's Overland*


Non-orbiting Forms, their nerves
tendrilling to lichen horns and eyelash,
prescribed rhythms in hips and hands
in the ritual
placement of cereals and wood — all

we pack with the solid geometry of kosmos
        through the deserts
to the tyrant of Persia.

All reduced to a speck
        in the lead hermeneut's right eye
and carried to the high yellow walls
on the east bank of the Tigris.

The dialogues, their commentaries,
        maps of psychagogic places

to which we travel, he and his companions, Harran's
        hive-shaped libraries and sparrow-back coloured clay temples.

Camel bells *tunk*, our robes fill
with dust.

*Tearing*


And Heraicus had become a Bacchus
as the dream had predicted
and a tearing rush swept through him
on skinny, hairy legs.
He became feathered with the Mysteries.
Like the woman Anthusa
he divined through cloud shapes,
weather's flesh, to see clearly the wickedness
of our Pamprepius, that vicious, unhappy soul
who laid a hand under the vested thigh of the Christian prince
Peter Mongus, a reckless
and remarkably evil man
and by this eyelessly woke torturers to stir
through double shifts in galleries
off Alexandria's alleys down that unfinishing year.

*Isidore on Philosophical Liberation*

Snowberries, corpse fruit,
rise, peaked on black stems,
plum bloom musters to sweep over us.

I dance as a crane
and lead congregants down to sing
in the well of the self's
cradle where as the song comes
from others' mouths
we eat it as food
we eat it as food
as snowberries stand
sharp on branches
and possible snow presses into skin
a bruise.
Thus, I taught the ceremonies
to the young Syrian rhetor,
Damascius, in
Horapollo's shining school
          in our Alexandria of the 480s.
I gave instruction in bird song and exact
movement of feet
in the theurgical theatres.

*Isidore at Prayer*


6:30 A.M. geese flying
to fields near the sea
pass through my heart
and inertia
of their night anchor places,
a swaying, watery
stability, passes through
my heart.
The flying group, that dart — *their weight,*
                              *their weight —*
lifts minutely to clear
at speed the mountain's west shoulder. Yi!
I, Isidore, perform all this
at certain moments in these Chaldean Rituals.

## Talking with the Mad King

The Dionysian state
of true philosophy
is maieutics and logic,
which produces such crystals as
Pythagoras and Iamblichus, winged
souls in the meadow of
divine forms, we say, pointing up.
'Men tend to bestow the name of virtue on a life of inactivity,
but I do not agree,' Damascius tells him. 'For the virtue
which engages in political activity
and discourse fortifies the soul.'
The beast clears his throat.
'That is why the learned, who sit in their corner and philosophise
utterly disgrace themselves if compelled to take some action.'
He snickers, treadling heavy legs below lap cloth
and coaxes a wad along pursed lips
as if it possessed foetal powers.
We brought him the Real. He sends the ball out,
emitted self-sprout, donated, mystical egg, to the crepuscular world.
We are half a month's walk from Harran
which sits inches inside the edge
of that empire that hates us.

*In 540*

We see him again
as he and his army maraud through towns
along the Sassanian-Roman border.

He drags clouds of prisoners
as if they make up
a bag full of kitchen junk
or a distended thorax; as if
made hideous by his piling notions, he's
become a gigantic grasshopper dragging
that belly across the sand.

He sells these people back to their families
and if money is not forthcoming
he kills his travelling guests and sometimes he kills
even after payment.

But when he comes to us in Harran
he cuts himself off from
the money poppy,
releasing all he'd taken, including Damascius's beautiful
Kurd servant Zosime 'because the majority
were not Christians.'

He's changed in other ways.
He is set on his horse by an ingenious pulley system,
loose skin at his neck quakes as he chews,
hair gone
bright blue from
burning northern forests.

*In the Throne Room*


How does the One move
and sound or run sand
through its hands? How occlude?
How does the One obey or reach
out its limbs?
Proclus indeed botched
the exegesis of *Parmenides* 157B, no
wire strung to the active
intellect, no liquefaction at the shore
of the speeches.
Daemons slash back and forth
as souls sling out
only to return, this the tidal
breath, from heaven
to earth then back, then down
again    cucumbers, snakes, cankers, moths
tumble in the ebb and flow with the man himself,
who now rocks, roaring and throwing his body in the daïsed, boar
skinned chair, caught in the net of spirit's
surf, as we all are, will, all shards, flammable dust,
his yanking lips, those muscular arms.

*Fear, Great Pneuma*


They murmur in the market of a 'century storm'
creeping near the coast,
monolith, motion's seething
jar, to card our cells about
to fall on us.
We urge fir
privately to whip us
roots farther
along rock.
Copper pipes in our houses
thin and tingle,
whistling.
Wind lifts,
off balance, still careful,
osprey dragging
giant rose fish from a spouting ocean.
The shore darkens in a stretched
oval biting panhandle, sea-entering glaciers,
wood smoke, low cloud brush
and among starfish
emulsifications in stacking fogs
callus crowns on judgment
and will rides out over
this berm residual discernment
bulbs before it
sliding on grease come from charm
untethered by the violent.

*Nothing*


Awake suddenly, 3:20 A.M., with
felted heaviness — what,
what — flaring, draped from collarbones,
or it was moss, thick, possibly flowing,
soft roar, inside, wake
feed the staring cat, eat myself.
Only later, in the back alcove,
in prayer, I see
how disarticulated my body is
in sole dark
still by the betrayal.
It was as if all the animals
passing through the yard
spoke eruptive Greek, hooks and sharps
sent flying,
with evil and efficient intent.
What weapons they'd created
found their routes (beat, teloi).
So it was shockingly novel.
So unbelievable as to be near
comedy.
You feel 'a kind of pity' says
Aurelius when people bend so
under the moon's crouched shadow.
You must hate
nothing.

*Simplicius Makes Out Mind in His Mind*


There you are in falling dark
                    pretty mouth, there
In those woods, in
Those breathing, yogic heights, fir tips swaying,
There you are little one, little,
Little peeper, there
Miles, there canyons,
Bread, love,
Lions, intertidal stones,
Ancient apple varieties, roses.
There walking up, there
Prince and quality, trembling stalk.


*Best sir, best Simplicius, I paced*
*Reptilian hills, running south the tongue*
*Of this long peninsula, walked, night journey,*
*Marsh marigold, walked*
*Bear's sleep,*
*Salmon's return,*
*To the stream walked*
*To the bell sound walked, walked*
*The aroma of low kitchens and lichen homesteads and the*
*Length of hummingbirds's feeding*
*And storms flickering — their*
        *teeth, their alert hair.*

*I traversed the mouth*
*Of the wolverine,*
*Fear's rickety bridge*
*With my fluent, undulant*
*Foot.*

*Priscianus*

I tell him once more
the mind brushing in
him, feeling a way,
is not his,
though its eye is kindly.

Eremurus pokes out a perfumed tongue
on scrapped mountains,
gladioli an orange smear
in diving crevasses.
Maples flare in flower and worms,
lime, eating wounds upward
through leaves
produce showers
of minute defecation.

*The Philosopher*


Acamatius, Hieropolitan,
*haruspex*, diviner and inspector
of still warm offerings, tight
with Groznyan hair-swept-back-from-the-forehead
pointmen, coastal medical
weed princes, explorer of the slushy gash in
hides of bulls, vocationally blood-soaked,
speaks prettily of Alkibiades, seal-skinned
favoured one, vogues him, aristo-mega, but with no phronesis
only foaming, coloured pertness and expressive
wrist watch flash, up to his elbows in condo
flips and charming in-flight-from-the-*gongan*-or-DEA
deals in Point Grey. He aims a cracking doom
muffler at the being's broadest muscle,
borrows a bank's million and vanishes
in an undertow of clean money.

He lifts the blood-ribboned
forehoof of the beast, measures
the wound and pronounces
the cut authentically
sacred. All the neighbourhoods
call him 'the philosopher.'

*Flash*

A whip of robins
sails across
the compound where he sends our food, then returns
damp winter air
soil darkening around its mouth.
The air would prefer rain
but is welded shut.
The birds flash to wake
some decision, decision.
I too wish to know
what lies behind halted air
see what animal is led from the stall
and watch for the slamming
birds to break a surface.
Sharp valleys widening
in cedars are in
on the secret, this is
sure, they twist
yet show nothing.

*Safety*


We hid the combing of flame from stone
under the large flake
of slate to the right
of the door to Damascius's gathering house.
There, too, the Aramaic grammars.

The psychopompic objects we wedged
in certain wells,
not silent but gaping,
as news of bright deaths of massed
coloured creatures in the sea
washed into the city and the academy,
the murmuring dormitories and classrooms
on the north slope of the Areopagus.

*Damascius, Remembering*


Hypatia, more noble
and far-going than her father,
the mathematician Theo,
held the stone not of this solar system;
infinitely beautiful, she wore the philosopher's
cloak and spoke on philia with anyone
in the sandy streets,
she whom the ecclesiarch Cyril
bull of the leading band had
men with arms of ground meat beat to death steps
from her home since many milled about her.
And there was Zeno
of limited intelligence
who drove a white ass through
the synagogue of Alexandria
and Salustius who asked
flustered Plutarch so many questions
he blurred the argument
and Nicholas the Orator, student
of Proclus
and Superianus the sophist
who came to learning quite late,
his ascetical scars shining
in the public baths
and the great Horapollo,
soul destroyer of Christians, cornered with kitchen knives
by seneschals of the envoy Nicodemus

in a room near his tall windowed lecture halls
in the terror of 488.

*Falling*


Gessius: physician supreme
under Zeno. He came from Petra
where star-chips in clouds rose
       through his sensorium's antlers and sandbar blond hair.
He met a holy woman blessed by
the gods with an extraordinary
nature. Pouring water into a
glass cup, she saw
the future braid and coagulate.
Crows flew up from falling
water, intentioned ash.

*What Must Be Done*


To Ctesiphon on the river, the nouns,
In obedience to Justinian's
Abolition of philosophy, in mammoth
Panniers on animals
Through endless sand, come.

In thin ebony boxes
Drivers hold on their laps
Singular equations
Like silvery exhalations of unimaginably
Graceful animals.

Proclus's commentary on
The *Parmenides*
Folded into three rhyming
Quatrains
Over which each pilgrim
Bends and draws
Into his flexing heart.

Assembly geometries
From Iamblichus's *De mysteriis.*

We set out at night
Under the intelligible stars.

All this to be atomised
And misted into weather
Systems of the throne's
Moods
In palace conversations
With Khusrau
In the dusky, laterite city.

## The Tongue

We urge him to dwell on sleep
and visions.
He is feverishly curious
and asks about celestial regions, tides and nearly
never sleeps, why reptiles
alone are poisonous though
he may stand as exception, winds'
colours, heat's and cold's
medical boons,
geometry's applications to war.
We propose the soul's tiny pink tongue
and what it likes.

His insanity is corrigible,
rockets with a range to
Constantinople streak overhead.

*Envoi: Answers to King Khosroes*

He becomes calmer.
When less troubled, he begins
The autobiography in which
Great lizards clear the roof
Of still-rising north east mountains to light
And arm him
Those whose loose hissing wings ripple
Fluidly in dreams.
His wife, breathy
Shill for Nestorians, propels currents
Through palace rooms and within
Them he finds himself calmer and mulls
Concordats on trade
In shimmering uranium ore.
He becomes calmer and gathers us
To stand before three questions on the soul
Its hard nature of course
Its homogeneous plaquing of every cranny
Then the deep linkage matter.
I mention Plato's bowl
In ur-time fever, unlikeness's deliria, where
Wave curl, rot, innumerability, wild
Celery flower, early universe arithmetical buds, whale lung spectacle-
    mash
Under the hammering pestle
Spouting the igneous human
Language, rainforest brain

And he bursts into Zoroastrian conflagration
And at the height of the burn, preternatural
Clarity and command on synaptic intentionality and meteorology
Stride toward him, him alone.

A moan
*Duduk* moan   nightly
From rocks, dried river beds.
At our elbow, Theophrastus's
*On Harmful Bites.*

*Actants, Conatus*

*Look, There —*


and the daemon
hair tied to one side, black,
    his sentness a creek dropping
        6,000 feet on stone, the caught-in-the-throat, the angel's
cold mind, now a dragonfly's
        livery and light armour, now a human smell, appears standing
in ferns
watching.

*Northeast of Creelman, Saskatchewan*

MOTHER

My brother and I end
up here, the stone house,
not ours really, belonging to
the English family, generations
gone, below Gooseberry Lake,
quarter inch frost on the inside face,
blue and yellow boulders,
roofless. Pelicans
jerky on water half a mile away.
We should, we know,
be head down and butting
in creek thickets of arithmetic
or at football practice.
We push through drifts, room to room, blood
reports, partly burned
photographs,
black corner brackets attached — we pass
staticy Geiger counter
hands over as on TV — bits
of machinery, energy ash
puffy around them.
Everyone gone, as we expected, mother, aunts,
uncle, driven out
to work at twelve, barefoot,
stooking behind the binders.

And staying out.
We think through this
but go looking for them anyway
coming back to fire pits
each late afternoon to set fresh
blazes.
Then Greg disappears, two-three weeks,
no word.

SING

Mother in the High River hospital,
bewitched by the watch-
like tracking device on her ankle,
just changed by the Nigerian
          — do you know Okigbo,
             I love you, you must —
nurse, re-diapered, exhausted,
waiting in the room that looks into
the top third of a gigantic cottonwood
for the loud woman, her mouth pointing
straight up to stop
yelling Help! Help!
waiting to return
to hymns
in the 'chapel'/ kitchen
she can't sing these days, is slotted,
keel driven onto sand,
in her wheelchair beside me, my
lostness, I'm all cloud and
wind, no use, no use
to her at all. She
tells me she is sad
when we sit later beside the hall
Christmas tree.
About what? All the defeats
in me.

The Depression, the war. Yes,
Yes. But the death of her
mother, little children sent
into winter fields
to look for lit windows,
cooking and cooking and cleaning for other
and other families.
Yet look!
snow! in the fenced
patio
though the word
leaps ahead of her
*bounding*
through drifts of itself —
*O O*
she holds the vowel
as other residents small bears.

*Deliverance from Error*


Orpheus — one of three caught
on snowy CCTV footage — forks
into loose blanched soil
expanding with a flick
in a single concussive puff just
below the surface, his flight-
blow strikes ringing wheat dust
cauling the battling combine;
it ignites, a passing shiver.
Inanna and Dumuzi, long Sumerian faces,
whicker in after, machine scrum whining
off, slowly blackening cloths,
advancing night, over their mouths, ether-soaked,
softening, sucking their god-bodies
in, interring them invisible in columns
of their own momentum.
The first reaches and touches
a nest of small boulders, music's
nativity point and a severed bear
tooth and lays a
palm on these. Error has accumulated
and dropped its sediment widely.
Keep sending them; next, I suggest, send al-Ghazali
with his bladed book or the fine kataphatic Suhrawardi.
Do keep sending them.

## Of the Harmony of the World

May sunlight
in the back, morning just clearing the high cliff, camas
stems yellowing, grass on the west slope dead, summer drought already on.

In the gulch on the top terrace, nothing much,
used up, rocks so sere, I sit in full
glow on the lichen-crusted green lawnchair left us by the previous
    owners,
leaves of a melanoma diagnosis open on my lap, *lectio*. Rocks
in the terrace quiet, sinking into knotted grass and dirt. Ocean Spray
a step from bloom. *Major Trends in Jewish Mysticism* or *Fusus al-hikam*
on the low, rusted table, tusked, beside a pillow clouded by worm
    droppings
raining from maples. How did I end up like this?

Beauty infiltrated everywhere.

Kepler in his crowing, ecstatic, incredulous opening to
'Of the Harmony of the World': 'I am stealing
the golden vessels of the Egyptians
to build a tabernacle for my God from them'; 'The very
nature of things was setting out to reveal
itself to men.' Just two: him and Ptolemy. Each on the end
of the charge from the sky's finger.

I curve below rock and break
stalks of dead grass. Hummingbirds swim overhead.

Any creature that God has not yet brought into existence is
    non-existent
though it certainly exists in some mode since it is an object
of God's knowledge. It is 'found' with God. (*Ibn 'Arabi's Metaphysics of
    Imagination*, William Chittick).

An alarming geometry
forces a winged trapezoid but rushing
so that mathematics because of drag melt, draining
along the crevices at the seams of the seen (seen, seen) lightly shaking
not-thereness that stands then rolls, then stands once more
in the non-patterned, non-ancestored, non-burning
but murderous bodiless light
folds of that pause, that wait, that complete
terrible that, that Greater Than Massive,
this new object swaddled in vision magma —
small gear, barley pearl, about to click into place
colour shift in northern bears as they slide
into trees or nil     novel shapes
of sadness.
Who can say?
We can't read
at all at this pitch.

An electrical fur for us
surrounds it
if we're very lucky.
And a gap where its heart could fit,
delay, gasp, oh, we provide
cloaked in flowing mud of a channel breaking up.

In that place walls
of wind-worked calculations,
where Shelley, our sweet emissary, bent toward
and below their eddies and buckles to ask the mother
of the new born for report on the doings
of the higher integers.
The eye of the world, burning,
pyramidic, gazing, quite
visible through the hole
in the number 4.

*Animal Set at the Centre of Unlit Oil Pots*


A boar with no obvious wound
sits in a rostrumed chair.
The theatre before him is dark aside
from his drained light directly
above the alert
if awkwardly seated
body.

Emptily-dark the theatre yet suffused with
quivery outlines of ears.
That dark yet stacked
with moist breathing.
The boar wishes nothing will be said
about what he reports,
nothing must be repeated
outside the room.

He's been to the Persian throne
and had explained to him what
will certainly come; he's been
to the northwest frontier.
He urges us to scratch out shallow pits in the ground.

*He Understands*


In this dream, the boar comprehends
the stone is moral.
There. Perfect Nature.
Emboldened 'I'
in flowing crest.
Energies, mercies, with lizard-like movements, sluice
through grass.
Trailing veils of mouth-smell,
tangled veils of neural maps
changing by the instant.
Burning oil pots are set around the animal
and then a further ring of flaming pots
goes around the extent
of his speech in the long hall.
The animal reads
from The Famine Book,
its lips moving
as they try to manage
the four tones.
Occasionally the creature
stops to make commentary
on nodes in the Tao te Ching.

*Via pulcritudinis*


Hummingbirds explode
overhead in halfdark
at the feeder, the time before
blooms. I eat porridge below.
Ravens shriek at fledglings,
ravens juggle extremely gravitied
joy in their drowning-in-
their-throats voices,
black brook of the raven's
hackling, spiney ora.

In the dream from last December, a plummet
through sky, accelerating past night's rim
odd flake slicing down
along night's horn
and at one hundred and fifty yards, we, cluster of fallers,
smell the animal-in-a-lair ground
in its vegetation as it comes in waves
out toward us, cowling, amouring us
piling wave.
Pinkish light wells through air.
Panes of ice on roads and
the plane from Seattle nosing
toward a ground impossible
to fully light.

The raven's cry a shield
or tomb cover
vaults our chests.
Is this what safety is?

Fires in the interior.
One late hummingbird
strikes a natalising course over drought
grass up the hill, stung
by, uncoiling, a new way of beauty.

*Nights*


They come after supper
Smoking rollies, in husbands' sweaters, overcoats,
And wait as their tubs fill,
A ratty, cozy smell of outhouses
Down the backlanes,
Benson School glowing in a limestone, fossiled shell,
Social Gospel's New Jerusalem to the west at the bottom
Of a soft rise.

The water from the standpipe
At the end of Princess Alexandra Street
Smells of beaver.
They pull their sleighs to it, the weedy water
Frozen on the runners and decks.

They're happy, stars
Dressed in skins and open-mouthed over them,
War over, no one made to claw fingers
Through stiff cod shovelled from freight cars now.
A few Chevrolets passing, their oxen bumpers and grilles.

They talk low, the water smells of jackfish
And bedroom slippers
And help sway coal carriers
And kid-washing basins
Off the soaked platforms
And over the wet pull ropes
Stamped into snow.

## Monuments and Marvels (patria et paradoxa)

*In the* Philosophical History *of Damascius, the literary genre* patria *concerns daily life in certain cities and at particular sites, foundational myths, accounts of monuments and local customs. Damascius is anxious to record as much of this as possible, since his tradition, as he put it, 'now stood on a razor's edge' following Justinian's abolition of philosophy in Athens and the disastrous relocation of the Academy to the court of King Khosroes of Persia.* Paradoxa, *equally important in elegy, records extraordinary occurrence. The woman amassing the marvellous instant below is the artist Amalie Atkins in* Listening to the Past/Listening to the Future, *2013.*

*

Along the Missouri River
   mound house scatters
dot the banks.
Ships at Fort Albany
claim shape in night
visions of the nun
in her small bed north of Green Lake.
Chaco canyon.
Ghost footings
of a library rising in Saskatchewan
to just above earth,
cargoed with the archives of the Second
Provisional Gov't at Batoche. Clovis.
Macchu Picchu.
Monte Verde

rib pole holes
by a stream in sub-Antarctic
Chile
signs of potato cultivation
and mastodon meat.
Buried houses
along a river's north
fork, called now 'The Milk,'
geese light in the Dakotas.

\*

Near the middle
of a frozen lake up
La Ronge way, days
within the boreal forest
flows a black
Victorian dress
in the liquid of wind.
Night decomposes, polish of pine light
on air's bone.
The woman holds
two dark funnels
at her ears, one
for the future (churning spot
sheds and gathers heat)
the other screwed tight
to the past.

Her face colour of ice.
She pitches into one
then the other, daemon
of attention.
Where could she have spent the night?

*Bonaventure*


His long black fern
      theology of three,
   his theory of knowledge a mouth, Augustine, huffing
warm moist air
        into our good, brown Franciscan wool
so within
   the cowl native plum muscles bloom
      fawn lilies lit from below, below-lit, forgotten-
lit, some source below sunken, networked
         roots of ivy, thus
with these powers given,
I deliver myself
to the stripping
of ivy from trees' torment —
ora et labora and apokatastasis.


Christ, reclining on his human
      and divine energies, their soft spines, performs in others' skins
        the agent intellect's hummingbird
          cruciform, midair dance, unspooling the intelligible pith
            from imagination's chilled phantasms.
You can see the original stain
   of these cranial ghosts
      where Ideas drained down from the higher sky
         blue like lines of sap.

The pear that has born a single
fruit over fourteen years
at the edge of my room
tingles with flower
in cold
cold, cold.

## Actants, Conatus

In these cold rooms, a few
steps into his *Quodlibetal Questions*, Duns Scotus tweaks
a lamp and makes appear across a wall, 'It is necessary
that the primary formal reason for just this
singularity stems from a thing
intrinsic per se to the singular
in question';
thus a fork appears on the teak table
shining like a boiling elf
just before I press the button
on the dishwasher door to start the cycle.
Advent 1306, University of Paris, warren of plastered
rooms, horse hair bound in the milky mix, smoke from fires in the streets,
Rue Coupe Gueule, gluey, rutted. He is in there
remarking on the particular, mote loosened
from the occultation of objects.
A fern of speech grows
on window glass.
So the thing rises in itself like a trout.
The Cowichan River untangles from mountains
along the large island's rain hump
to coil through corn and grape fields, away from clearcut.
The water, in enclausteration, in the veil of being
beyond its name, moral power, peels back —
                    what? Just what does it pry
and draw back like a lid precisely? — and displays the
                              stepping forth skin,

tight with gravity thing-pit, forehead
peering jewel, it itself and what's left of corn tassel, grape
burgeoned, odd standing fir or alder
with wind alone around it, dangerous, iris-like stuff
there, each speck lunging inside
classical form, at which for quite a while
I have been aimed in flying marriage.
Light is not dug out of a thing by a thing
tearing at itself with its claws.
It can't or won't do this.
Dishwasher, the fires. No.
Nor is it left back, lost in seeing's slag
but gets punched or pillowed up, spruced, burnished by water.
So that it stands up. Or slants toward. Appears in a mouth
filled with tiny, near-invisible, conscious hairs. What
it does.
Who would have guessed?
Then it is that lone fir, fork, caked lick
of mane hair
presents a piece of paper,
causing it to slide across teak laminate
under the spectral hand of the Angel's mind,
written on it your own simple name.

*The Light of the World*


The mountain's grey float
            metaphysical curtain rising
The mountain's heavenly apartments
The mountain's Anhui Provinceness
There, see people bent at the waist so high
                        pulling brome
The mountain is a wet-brown armoured horse
            turning its head
The mountain rises and sleeps backward
        into the corral of a cloud-doped sun
The mountain in performance
    in the suit of a spectacle name
The mountain refuses, it
            is not terraced for tea-planting
or ivy bed
The mountain TEXEN
The mountain     deer, their
            smart, spherical, occult beds
The mountain's nursery
        of names
            your own too at the piney milk
The mountain     snowberry
            (step back, cadaver fruit)
The mountain     yellow, blue and dun rock

The mountain's bullion
        of waiting
stamped with grape-clustered un-names
before-names
Mountain cleaving

The cliff is a tongue
    and what it says you receive at your own
          tongue's unkenable root
The path you are on, its substance, be confident it
is utterly deniable
The mountain's bushy fern
        coat
The mountain all that can be
        plausibly denied
heaped
The mountain, do not talk of it
Do not seek it or ask
of it a word
The mountain's updraft
height pulls
your hair
The mountain in gorges
the mountain    hummingbirds' final cause
The mountain    forbs
    and moss around rock
creating a painted eye

which looks at Val Plumwood
        where she, seal flash, thought
and fluoresced     Or Gillian Rose
The mountain     ginger ferns
                blue-eyed grass
Lurking, certain, simple
            reckless and admirable camas bulbs
hold steeped in ground
The mountain's breast to the sea


Soak this in water, alder leaf
stained water and pocket the remains under sod flap where oaks
    slanting cliffwise
lay their tops on a small plateau.

*Pathos*


Aelred of Rievaulx listens to me,
He shifts and angles his cocked, spread-display ears toward me,
Rufous towhees, bloodflecked at the core, stalking,
On through dry leaves, ambulancing, dragging what?, the hearing,
Twelfth century, comes through alder grove of static,
Which is the claw scritch of arthritis,
And through several yards of iron, the man's complete death.
Sleep is everywhere
In his gravity-drenched monastery,
North England —
His hearing wolves in, lilacs in —
I hold my tongue,
The listening works over.

*West of Nanaimo, Poverty and Variety*


duct metal ice
or quarter inch thicker
lead soldered tin on
a third of the lake
then gelatinous film and black trapdoor
water
fir trunks angling equally
through heavy and hardly
there ice
and cloud pushing down the
snowy fir smudged
pre-dawn mountain
nearly to thinnest ice, bird's
transparent lid.
woodpecker   winter
wren   owl rustle in theatric gloom
cedar
ice on the path foot
burnished snow
snow crumbs whip
at daybreak watched from a
halfdark kitchen
the Dipper emptying above the roof.
(cougar's single print
in mud northside
of the lake where sun clears
the mountain)

John of Kanty's day,
Dec. 23, lecturer in theology
Augustinian, 14th century, Krakow, floor
sleeper, unjustly fired,
his blackened tibia in a boat
turning on the Vistula.
ruby-throated hummingbird
coated with tremor
sucks in tiny beats
a globe of pine sap
what can be freed
there my cheek

## The Beach, the Wall


*The chorus of the right hand sings:* Jack Blaylock broke his leg
A day before his bunch took in
The Dieppe raid, Green Beach,
Cecil Last down.
Most of the boy's side of Sequin School in the water.
*The chorus of the left hand sings:* he had a sooty look in bars and
    poolhalls
In Windthorst and Kipling.
Still smelled of rhubarb leaves and early frost.
The stare, but avoiding your eye.
*The chorus of the right sings:* he smelled
Of loose stones, the push of incline, the wall.
Big cut on his upper lip when
He passed through barbed wire
On a sleigh on a calf-pissed-on hill with his sister.
*Chorus of the left hand:* burned hair reek of him from being worked
That way by doorframes.
Too drunk to do much, but the face,
As he turned it, said he'd achieve
Real damage if he ever got an actual bead.
*Chorus of the right:* he married the beautiful Edna Uppold.
House, garden to the road.
Cleanest summerfallow around.
Ground swinging back freely on its hinges
For him, it seems, alone.
*Chorus of the left:* a tear of ivy shade
Under his tongue, driving back from town, 71,

Ivy under his tongue, new license for the truck, heart,
Half ton sliding softly
Across new gravel, kneeling,
The lord of the opposite ditch rising
Extending an obsidian ring.

## Red Dawns, Forests Burning

I suck the tongue which is
      presented to me as a spigot,
and from the Corybant flies colostrum
      flowers, miles, flammable hills
arcing through my skin.
And along this parabola's injection I climb
into his eyes and from there enter his farthest mouth
smell the origin of his breath then
occupy his fingertips.
I am the desert colour his skin hid
I am the roots, little bulbs
of his hair
I touch the curves of his speech
before it brushes air
And within him I hunt
the lightgoosebumped city that spreads inside him
I go down every street and through squares
And then, dusk deepening, light a skinny fire
part way up an undeveloped draw
risking all
and chose for myself a
form of life.

*'Our nature is at present a* tenebrosa substantia
*but it is capable of light. Light itself.'*

John Scotus Eriugena

From this coiling mass, weight of darkness
  you carry juniper lamps.
The murderous Light exists,
but does not dwell in this telephone code
thank god.
In these parts, God is 'stone in stone.'
Reading Eriugena is being slightly drunk.
Reading Eriugena is flying
a cargo plane (marbles of The Talking
Shop on pallets, all the blue voices, inside) a force
keeps pulling down,
mountains spreading in the windscreen
then an unseeable valley;
there we aim
— breath's window.

*In the Yard*


Yes, Eriugena — lovely man. Haven't looked at his *Periphyseon* in
over a decade, but loved
his knee weakening hand-speed and weave.
So, I suppose, pitter-patter, let's get at it
and set out nets, light, shimmery grey, with gigantic panes, at dusk,
blowing, attached to trees
for an interior scent
to occupy before the flowing, swelling
castled face of catastrophe.
It shall be yellow and of course furtive.
The doe with the shoulder wound
and her two fawns and red geraniums on the half wall hold
the yard to the ground and force it to be
the covey
I stack myself in.
Then I see
the bank's
full and coming over the sides.
Eriugena? Maybe. Fackenheim, Peter Maurin.
Smell of flame having passed over them.

*St. Peter's Abbey, July 2016*

I

The sky carries sea monsters
rising shapes from the choir's highest voices
as a Cessna releases gusts of
            desiccant over canola.
Water in fields latches at clouds.
The elderly Dominican at breakfast
on the eve of Bonaventure's
feast reveals the church
falls in Quebec.
Spruce goatee, pointy white
cowl at vespers yesterday.
Set hermeneuts to gaze
into vapour
unsheathed by the plane.

II

That tremble in a haycutter wheel
with a shot bearing. So fares the interior eye
        making its way.
Twenty year olds, gambling two million
a year, slide from truck cabs before the Pharmasave,
barley fallen between here
                    and Nipawin
under head-weight of water.
Bonaventure swims over levers of imagination
to seed and bring down worlds.
Town of Carrot River drowned in
seven inch rain, dogs plucked
in rowboats and front end
loaders before the Co-op and Petro-Can.

III

Sadness in abandoned
farmhouses south of Liberty, Sask.
through that nearly white soil,
purple, unfixable worth.
Chrome kitchen set, grey
green plastic cushions
pushed into a corner.
How to weigh dust on the eye, disinter spoon
tick in coffee, in 1956
a name called down stairs?
Caragana seed pods crack
over mottled cement;
in the east, earth curves
to marshes along the mud lake.

IV

The soul born to know
                    everything
sticks at its rim
                    and saddens
in natura; the angel
                    opens
no mouth in *De scientia Christi.*
To know anything know
the constitution of the divine serum, this
beyond all.
Clover stupefied, huge in ditches,
with hawkweed, brown
eyed susans, is struck by near-liquid
clubs of bees.

*Notes*

Poems in this collection have previously appeared in *Granta* ('The Light of the World' (as 'There Is No Light of the World But the World')), *Reliquiae* ('Isidore, Pedagogue,' 'A Mountain Floats Before Us,' 'Isidore of Philosophical Liberation,' 'Simplicius Makes Out Mind in his Mind,' 'Safety,' 'Damascius Remembering,' and 'What Must Be Done') and *Arc* ('Deliverance from Error'). Many thanks to the editors.

I wish to acknowledge the help provided me by Polymnia Athanassiadi's *The Philosophical History of Damascius*, especially her introduction and notes.

*

3   'SN̲, AK̲E' is a SENĆOŦEN word meaning 'Snow Mountain'.

8   'Men ... soul' / 'That ... action', SOURCE: Polymnia Athanassiadi, *The Philosophical History of Damascius*, Apamea Cultural Association, 1999. ISBN 9789608532526.

9   'because ... Christians', SOURCE: *Ibid.* Every effort has been made to trace the copyright holder and to obtain their permission to republish these excerpts.

37  'I am ... men', SOURCE: Johannes, Kepler, *The Harmony of the World*, (E.J. Aiton, A.M. Duncan, J.V. Field, (trans.)), 1997. ISBN 9780871692092. Permission courtesy of the American Philosophical Society, with special thanks to Mary McDonald.

38 'Any ... God', SOURCE: William C. Chittick, *The Sufi Path of Knowledge: Ibn 'Arabi's Metaphysics of Imagination*, 1989. ISBN 0887068855. Permission courtesy of the State University of New York Press, with special thanks to Sharla Clute.

51 'It is ... question', SOURCE: John Duns Scotus, *Quodlibetal Questions*, (Felix Alluntis, Alan B. Wolter (trans.)), 1981. ISBN 0813205573. Permission courtesy of the Catholic University of America Press, with special thanks to Brian Roach.

62 'Our ... itself', SOURCE: John Scotus Eriugena, *Periphyseon: The Division of Nature* (I.P. Sheldon-Williams (trans.), John O'Meara (ed., trans.)), 2020. ISBN 9780884024620. Permission courtesy of Dumbarton Oaks Publications.

Ingram Content Group UK Ltd.
Milton Keynes UK
UKHW020619060423
419743UK00013B/544